UNDER
THE
CATALPA
TREE

By: Paula Julson

While every precaution has been taken in the preparation of this book, the publisher assumes no responsibility for errors or omissions, or for damages resulting from the use of the information contained herein.

UNDER THE CATALPA TREE

First edition. December 29, 2024.

Copyright © 2024 Paula Julson.

ISBN: 979-8230013426

Written by Paula Julson.

Table of Contents

Title Page.. 1

Introduction 6

The Reveal.. 9

First Impressions 17

Lend Me Your Ear 23

Abundance 30

Things can only get worse.............................. 38

Friendly Fire.. 46

Soul Mates.. 53

The Party Never Stops 61

WHY? 68

Even Warriors Die 80

What We Remember 89

Introduction

If there was ever such a thing as a redo in life, I would want one with you. I would savor the time we spent together and never take for granted all the silly moments and all the unimportant things that I would unknowingly wish back one day. I know now that you were part of my growing and healing process, and I'd like to think that I was instrumental in yours. You helped release the woman I am now, that was hidden inside for years before you. You taught me to trust again. You opened my eyes to all the good things a person can be. I discovered how fun it is to have friends. *Real* friends.

I see now, how every minute counts. Every thought. Every word. Every action. They all tie in to one another and in the end, it all makes sense. In friendship, the years fly by, and yet time stands still, and we never dream it will run out one day. You taught me to love myself. My weird hyper and more than often, dramatic self. I found my voice, and I learned how to say no to the things I didn't want in life. I hope the suffering you endured during your lifetime made you the richest bitch in heaven. I feel in my heart that you are rewarded with anything you have ever wanted. I can't wait to see your face and hear your laughter. If you can, please save a seat for me, so I can sit next to you once again.

If ever there is tomorrow when we're not together, there is something you must always remember. You are braver than you seem, and smarter than you think. But the most important thing is,

UNDER THE CATALPA TREE

even if we're apart, I'll always be with you. AA Milne

1

The Reveal

Grief. It has a way of revealing who people really are. The definition of the word, is to describe a deep sorrow, usually caused by someone's death, but can also describe a feeling caused by an annoyance, or something found to be upsetting. I was experiencing both definitions today. The unbearable heat, mixed with the relentless bloodsucking insects were causing me grief, while my heart ached from the loss of my dear friend. While the numbness from the reality of it was settling in, I still had to giggle to myself at the thought of the gentlest creature on earth deciding to put us all through it in the end. As I sat there in my silent misery, I surveyed the small crowd starting to gather around her beautiful smiling face propped up on a table in front. It was one of her best photos taken. She looked so vibrant and full of life. Then, out of nowhere, a wave of nausea came over me. I blamed it on the intense heat, added with the realization of losing her. Was it all worth it? Was this fucking it? Is this what everything she went through in her life amounted to?

Suddenly, my mind wandered back to a text she sent me a few months before she passed. Word for word it said, "People crawl out of the woodwork whenever someone dies, proclaiming their special relationship." "I think many times it's true, while other times it's disgusting and a bid for attention." She went on to name a few people, who were sitting here today, and how she hadn't seen, or heard from them in months. And yet, here they are now, just like she predicted, eager to be seen and heard today.

Then, to make matters worse, I noticed him sitting there in the second row. The row usually reserved for immediate family only. Why did he think he deserved a reserved seat? All he ever did was go out of his way to make her life miserable.

I can just imagine the look of loathing and disgust I had on my face, had he looked over his shoulder. We never made eye contact, although he had to of felt my eyes burning holes into his back.

He sat motionless while silently absorbing everything being said about her, and her abbreviated life, as if he'd never known her. His expression never changed. Like a stone wall, he sat listening to the praises of the most amazing woman I had ever known.

I wanted to rip his heart out of his chest for disfiguring hers. I wondered, if he had any remorse for the things he did and didn't do. By the looks of it, no. It made me seethe at the thought of him sitting there in that intimate space blending in with the people who adored her. Sure, they had history, but he burned that bridge and no longer belonged there. He was taking a seat away from someone who would give anything to have her back here with us.

I found myself trying to hold it together in that beautiful space she had chosen as her final resting place. I hated him for stealing the beauty away from this sacred moment. I hated myself for hating him. I hated that God made this day we gathered in her name, so miserable that we couldn't find any peace in any of it.

I felt her presence with every gifted breeze on that stifling afternoon. I wondered if he did too. Such a waste. Did he ever love her? Will he ever know how disappointed she felt in him not stepping up his game, in being the greatest man of her life? If he loved her, did he ever try and make it known? Did he ever beg her not to leave him? Will he ever truly know just how much she wanted to stay and love him? How could someone as passionate as she was, ever give herself to such a cold and lifeless man?

I wanted to leap from my chair and knock him off his. How dare he sit there with that look on his face pretending to care. He didn't fucking care. He had the boys all to himself now. They had nowhere else to go, but back to him. How convenient.

The sound of my heart pounding out of my chest, drowned out the meaningful melodious lyrics being sung. I could feel the rage rushing through my veins with every beat. My eyes stung with sadness but never shed a tear. I was too disgusted with it all. Why did I even care so much? It wasn't my life, it was hers. Why did I feel the need to avenge her, even after her story ended? Why was I so affixed on him and his last act? And an act it was. Was I the only one to see through it? Were all these people oblivious of all the sleepless nights and tears she spent on this man? Had they forgotten all lost conversations, and how she begged him for the bare minimum but was never considered important enough, by his standards, to receive it.

She invested everything she had into those boys and spent her last 15 years making sure they oozed the love she poured into them. She gave them the gift of laughter. She gave them a lifetime of experiences they would have never known with him. She opened the window to the world around them, and in doing so, she also opened the door to creativity and imagination. The world was no longer his way or the highway. She gave them the power to decide on who they wanted to become and the freedom of choice.

Will they ever know how hard she fought for the right to raise them her way? How he constantly tried to trip her and drag her back with every step she took? She was his possession and nothing more. Until death do us part, or more like for his better, and her worse. Was it my job to make it known? Was it my job to pull back the curtain and expose him and a few others sitting here today? Would she want me to even do such a thing?

Perhaps, I felt compelled because her children were robbed of unconditional love. They would never again feel the safety and warmth of her home. They will only have memories of her laughter. Of someone who truly knew their wants and needs, and willingly tried everything within her power to make them happen. Who gave them the courage to speak up and be heard.

Why would they allow him to sit here as if he was her friend? As I watched his emotionless efforts, I caught some movement out of the corner of my eye. Of course...her mother.

With face in hands, inching her way to her chair. Another class act. Another well-kept secret she diligently fought to keep. How she was constantly distracted and tormented by this woman's tactics for attention. No one sitting here will ever know the many times she had to step away from her life to save this person who called herself "mother." They would never know how much effort she put into trying to save this woman from her addiction, her bouts of depression, and acts of "helplessness". All while dealing with her ex's barrage of good 'ole boy bullshit.

I remember reading the several paragraphed text messages her mother would send that went into insane detail about dreams of suicide and depression, while she, herself, was fighting to stay alive from her cancer riddled life. The selfishness displayed by her own flesh and blood, made it unable to look at her with compassion.

I'm not one for empathy. I will not walk a mile in someone else's shoes just to know how they feel. Perhaps the tears her mother shed, came from regret for the way she treated her daughter. Maybe, she really was mourning the loss of her daughter, and not thinking of her own well-being, now that the only person who tried to help her is gone.

I couldn't help but relive the relentless stress that my friend had to deal with ever since I came to know her. The memory of the look on her face as she was telling me her story. How is one to remain positive and resilient, when these people, as her family, were supposed to be the ones protecting her, and did everything they could to make her life a constant battle? I remember it all. I saw it. I heard it. And I can't forget it.

As I watch her mother's award-winning presentation of crippling sorrow and despair, I couldn't help but think her as helpless as ever. But she wasn't helpless. That's what people didn't understand. She just craved the attention and knew how to get it. As I watched her take her seat in front of the ex-husband, I almost said aloud, "how perfect!" The two main characters in creating her chaos, together at last.

I could feel the sweat forming a river down the middle of my back as I inched forward in my seat. I told myself that I needed to settle down before I had a heart attack. RELAX! I decided to turn off my brain and try to soak in all the beauty that surrounded me. Aside from the intense heat, the location she picked was picturesque. She always did love the surrounding countryside that enveloped our small universe we called home. The huge

catalpa tree was glorious in stature. I had never seen a most peculiar tree as this, with its massive trunk, and sprawling branches that eerily reached out towards us, as if to embrace us in our sorrow. It was breathtaking. I thought, how fitting, that we sit under the shade of such a species imperfectly beautiful as she was.

I wish I could see her face again. I would give anything to hear that sweet raspy voice and infectious giggle. I could almost smell her scent of essential oils wafting in the air.

As I sat there, I could slowly feel the panic rise into my throat. How was I going to get through the rest of my life without my dearest friend? Who was I going to confide in and laugh in secrecy with? No one else knew me like she did, and I didn't want them to. She was the only one I wanted. And now she was gone.

I wanted to cry with everyone around me but refused out of anger. Angry that she had to deal with everything she went through in life and death. What was it all for? Will it all be forgotten in a couple months' time?

They talked of her strength and how hard she fought to stay alive. Of course she did! She loved her life even though it was less than desirable by most standards. Fuck this! It can't end here. I refuse to stop saying her name. Everyone sitting here needs to hear her side of the story. Why should her offenders walk away untouched by karma? People deserve to know how often she resurrected herself from her crippling life just to make others feel loved. I promise she will be remembered.

In my defense, they should have treated her better. She wasn't at fault for their chosen behavior. She died a lamb thrown to the wolves. Am I to worry about their privacy? Their feelings? That won't even enter the playground. Let them display their act of sorrow today, because tomorrow will be hers.

2

First Impressions

I can't remember ever seeing her face or hearing her name before she came into the store that day. I was working for a local cellphone company, and we were already stretched thin, so I'm sure my attitude was front and center. I remember she had her boys with her, only they were very young. Her youngest had to have been only six years of age. Wow...I can't believe that much time has already gone by. I don't remember what I was doing when she walked in, but I somehow ended up helping her with her request.

I had to look up her account in our system, and to do that, I needed the name of the person who did most of the business with us. She told me that probably would've been her husband. I punched in the last name and three accounts with different first names showed up on my screen. I called out the first name among the three listed. I barely got out of my mouth, when I heard "he's dead" come from hers.

What a way to make a first impression. She was frustrated as it was, having to wait until someone wasn't busy to help her, and then having all the kids with her, just added to her frustration. The way she said it was enough for me to understand how she was feeling at that moment. She looked at me like I was the dumbest bitch around because I already didn't know that he was dead.

I felt the heat start to warm my cheeks and prayed that I wasn't visibly red. Who was this man whom she declared dead?

Someone close? Come to find out, it was her husband's brother who they found hanging in a tree on the family farm. Recently, I might add. Go me! And in front of the kids! Ugh!

I quietly went on to find what she was looking for without a word, and we politely went about our business and went our separate ways. I never saw her again, until a year later.

I since quit that job and went to school to get a degree of some kind, in hopes of improving my life. Or so I thought.

What I was really trying to carry out, was to impress my then boyfriend, who acted as if I didn't exist. Little did I know that all my hard work would go unnoticed. Both semesters on the Dean's List, with 33 credits in nine months' time, but no job experience in the field that I was climbing that mountain for. That meant no dream job. Or at least the job he wanted me to have. So, I did what everyone else in my small town did... I got a job at the local factory. Hey, it paid more than my last job and it gave me more flexibility. Plus, it allowed me to move out of his house and get a place of my own.

I remember the day so vividly. The day my whole world changed. I was outside on my break having a cigarette, when she came around the corner to do the same. Shit. I wonder if she remembered who I was? I remembered her, so I'm damn sure she remembered who I was. The silence was awkward as hell. I pretended to be busy with my thoughts and didn't dare look at her, for two reasons. I didn't want her to realize who I was, or if she already knew, I was sure she didn't want anything to do with me.

I don't know if it was the fact that we were the only two out there, and she felt as awkward as I did, or she just wanted to be the bigger person and say something to break the ice, so she complimented me on my outfit. I did look pretty put together that particular afternoon, with my cute pink and brown argyle sweater, pink earrings and of course, a pair of smart looking loafers to match. But I took her surprise compliment as generic, because that's what women do when they don't know what else to say. They comment on your hair, or your clothes. Either way, I was taken aback and smiled the weakest smile, and said thank you as I took the last drag off my cigarette and went back inside. Thank God that was over. The longest ten minutes that ever existed.

I look back now and laugh at what she was probably thinking as I walked away. "We meet again, bitch". Guaranteed!

I found out later, that she was well known at that factory. She already had thirteen years under her belt, and they gave her a special job. She was what they called a "specialty shopper", which meant if someone didn't know for sure how the material felt, or what the true color was of an item of clothing, they called her with any questions before ordering.

She was pretty much secluded in some room lined with shelves, that held every item they sold online. So, the only time I ever ran into her was on my cigarette break. And we were pretty much the only two out there every damn time! After a while the awkwardness started to fade, and we offered some light conversation to one another, but kept it short and sweet between drags off our cigarettes. I'm not sure how much time went by before we agreed to meet at the local watering hole after work. I should mention that my then boyfriend, owned the place. It was there the friendship started to blossom into something much more than a work relationship.

It seemed we had more than a few things in common. Our

dysfunctional childhoods, our crazy mothers, and our seemingly never-ending attraction to emotionally unavailable men. We were both raising three sons the best we could, with our exes breathing down our necks, ridiculing every step we took without their guidance. Guidance...yeah, that's what we'll call it.

She would tell me what he was doing to sabotage her efforts to break free, and I would share my experiences under similar circumstances I had during my two divorces. TWO divorces. Go me!

I remember how pissed off I used to get listening to her. How can a woman so seemingly strong, be so weak and not fight back? Why was she allowing this man to manipulate her this way?

I've seen pictures of him, and in my opinion, he wasn't that captivating to put anyone in a chokehold like he was doing to her. But, then again, she would giggle at the attraction I had to the man I was with at the time. Touché...fair enough.

The phrase "Beauty is in the eye of the beholder" rings true. To me, he just looked like the average mullet wearing redneck living in the backwoods surrounding our little town. They seemed to be plentiful. Every country girl's dream. Whatever...

Maybe, that's why I fell for the man I was currently seeing at the time. There was nothing "small-town" about him. He was small in stature, but big on living large. He saw the big picture. He dreamed big and wanted to see the world. He introduced me to many first-time experiences that I never would have been introduced to, if it hadn't been for him. He didn't discriminate, when it came to race, or sex. It didn't matter who you were, or where you came from. He felt as if you were ultimately the one to oversee your own destiny. You just had to work for it, then do it.

Whereas, my friend's "man", believed women were only created to keep men satisfied and happy, while taking care of everything else. I saw him as somewhat lazy. She was the breadwinner in my eyes. Homeschooling all her children, working full-time at night, plus running a successful side business. What the fuck was he doing besides living off her loyalty and low self-esteem? He used it to his advantage to get what he thought he deserved. And it was working.

Men found her beautiful and easy to be around, so she had no problem finding someone to cure her loneliness but would always fall back and revert to what he believed her to be...his.

I made it my mission to "save" her from this man. To drill into her head all the wonderful things that I saw in her and make her feel capable of living without the same life-giving air that he was sucking out of her.

I can't explain it. I compare it to what people refer to as a "soul mate". It was more than a friendship. I felt as if I had subconsciously known her for years before we even met. We became inseparable. She would look for me as soon as I got to work, and I would wait for her private messages after I clocked in and got online. Which was a no-no, but we would do it anyway. That's just how we rolled. No one was going to tell us what we could, or couldn't do, ever again. Or so we thought.

3

Lend Me Your Ear

Why is it when we find that special someone that we can connect with, we try to cram as much information about ourselves into them all at once? There is no way they can process it all, and a lot of it goes in one ear and out the other. We pick and choose what we deem important enough to remember, and the rest we pack away into that storage closet hidden in the back of our mind. Only now, I can remember some of the things that I put in there almost fifteen years ago.

We would be content to just sit for hours and talk about our lives. We'd never mention the weather, or the daily news. We wouldn't even talk, or gossip about anyone else all that much. Although, we did like to discuss our ex's attempts at replacing us, and how no one could hold a candle to what they once had. There was no earthly way they could ever replace us.

The conversations would mostly be about our unwanted past, our current wants and needs, and our future hopes and dreams. The aspirations that we honestly believed we would obtain one day because of all the suffering we had already gone through. I genuinely hoped all of them would have happened for her, because she seemed to want it more than I did. All I wanted was revenge for all of the broken promises, where she just wanted to be loved by someone who adored her.

Truth be told, I just didn't give a shit anymore. After surviving two failed marriages and living day to day in my current dysfunctional arrangement, I didn't see the rainbow anymore, let alone the pot of gold at the end of it. But she always saw the pot of gold. She made it seem that all our efforts were worthwhile.

My problem was, I didn't know how to reinvent myself. I couldn't jump from this crazy rollercoaster I've been on since I graduated high school. I was just relieved to know that there were other women on the same ride as I was, so I didn't feel so broken.

We would get together every chance we could and grab a drink, head to the beer garden, and light up. Our messy little lives would disappear, and we would get lost in Shakira's "Hips Don't Lie" playing on the jukebox. If we were together, we had everything under control.

Her laughter was addicting, and I started to crave it. I don't know who she inherited it from, but I'd never heard anyone laugh like she did. I was always jealous of people who could laugh so easily. It just seemed to effortlessly roll out of her mouth and touch everyone within an ear's shot. People would stop and turn to see where that contagious laugh was coming from.

I also didn't realize I was that hilarious, until I met her. She found my "I don't give a fuck" attitude humorous. She never once told me to change it. I saw myself as angry, and bitter, but apparently, she found it endearing.

Opposites attract. But aside from her friendlier approach, I found that we were quite similar in character. We were the caretakers in life. We talked ourselves into believing that no one else in the whole world could do what we were doing, any better than we could. Our purpose was to take care of our family and deflect all the crazy shit being drilled into them. We weren't afraid for our own well-being. We just wanted better for our kids.

We found it necessary to decipher the bullshit being handed out by our exes and see through their bag of magic tricks used in trying to lure our children over to their side. We were the protectors, and there was no way in hell we were going to allow them to manipulate or brainwash our flesh and blood and ruin them like they tried to ruin us. Sounds a bit dramatic, but at the time it is what we vehemently believed.

I never had a partner in crime before. Oh, sure, I had friends in the past, but no one I didn't have to pretend to. I had one other true friend that I could trust, and that was pretty much it. I was raised to believe that I had to always be on my best behavior to keep friends and make others love me. But I found a small circle where I could be authentically weird and obnoxious. We could say anything to each other and still remain close.

As mentioned earlier, I believe that she was my soulmate. She was the greatest relationship that I will ever experience in my life. She knew me inside and out, and no man could come close to what I had with her, and they knew it. It was us against the world!

Even though she still enjoyed a man's company more than I did at the time, she knew that I was safe to tell all the torrid details of her late-night escapades to. I still hold secrets that will never cross my lips.

I found myself living vicariously through her, when it came to braving the opposite sex. She was vivacious and had a wild side that came out with the captain and diet she would always drink. I too, liked to flirt, but found it impossible to stay interested in anybody longer than one night. She had no problem braving a first date or hookup. She was a trusting soul who always had such high expectations with every flirtatious meeting, but when she got them alone, they would show their true creepy selves and we would piss our pants laughing, as she painted a picture of the reality on how the night ended.

She was a lot braver than I was. She knew she was letting herself down every time she got involved with these trial runs, but she seemed to be having fun with it at the time. I, on the other hand, sat in disbelief at some of the things she revealed to me the next day, and could never again look that man in the eyes knowing what I knew. But she didn't care, and neither did I. As women in our 40s, we'd pretty much seen and heard it all by now, so nothing really shook us up anymore.

I remember the warm night air, mixed with her essential oil blend and the smell of burning tobacco. I thought those nights would go on forever. I didn't want anything more than what I already had. I felt safe and loved. I looked forward to every day. Who cares if I was living paycheck to paycheck. Who cares if my ex was breathing down my neck watching my every move and trying to turn my kids against me. Who cares if my boyfriend was a selfish prick who only knew I existed when he felt horny. None of it mattered. The world and all its problems could just fuck off. Everything was going to work out. I was living one day at a time, and for once in my life, I was in love with who I was then and there.

I began to realize that I wasn't unlovable, as I always thought I was. I learned that I didn't have to be someone I really wasn't, just to impress people that didn't really care. All those years of trying to force myself on fake friends, and for what? I couldn't stand to be around any of them!

I finally had a tight circle that consisted of only four women. Four glorious women that I know would be there at any moment if needed. Four resilient, loving, and authentically raw women, that I wouldn't trade for anything. People that kept my secrets. Who listened without judgment and understood, because we were all going through it together. We were invincible. I still respect every one of them yet today, and I'm still amazed at their strength.

I felt alive! I began to embrace my individuality that made me who I was, and realized I held the power to change my destiny. I stopped waiting on a man to fulfill my dreams, and realized he was never coming to save me. I had to save myself. Being with these women made me realize we all make mistakes, but it is our job to correct what is wrong. To stop repeating history and leap from the rollercoaster leading to nowhere.

We all made the decision to end our crappy marriages and forge a better way of life for us, and our children. We dared to seek out real relationships with people who listened to what we had to say and cared about our feelings. We were more than sexual objects that cleaned the house and fed the kids. We were people with dreams and wanted more than what we were offered. We wanted what we were promised.

The weak promises given in haste, just make us stay in a world that offered us absolutely nothing. We were expected to submit and be thankful. To be satisfied with what we already had and dare not dream of anything more. To except our lives as if it were meant to be this way. Fuck that! We knew better!

As women who have faced the devil in our times of need, we knew there was a better life waiting for us. We did everything expected of us, and we were going to get exactly what we deserved. Our freedom. If we had to ruin our livers to get there, so be it! We decided that it was better than sitting at home watching them sleep in the recliner.

We were like a pack of wolves out for the hunt. In search of our independence and our right to our own lives. We wanted to dance near the fire and feel the heat. We wanted our blood to ignite our bodies and keep us warm through the cold nights. We longed for passion and first experiences. All the things we missed in our first forty years, because someone we loved told us we could live without it.

We vowed to live in our cheap and rundown apartments and work our dead-end jobs, so that we would have the freedom to be the women we always knew we were. Wild and undomesticated. Mysterious and aware. Sexual and uninhibited. We weren't afraid to brave the obstacles that leapt from the shadows. We would never admit that we were wrong in leaving our "happily ever after" to start over again. We would do whatever we had to do, to show those that once hurt us, they should nary dare to try it again. We became the example of what happens when you lie to a woman.

4

Abundance

I went through many changes within the first ten years after my second divorce. I didn't even recognize who I was anymore. Who was this party girl that worked hard and played even harder? I became more outgoing. I was no longer tight-lipped and became more outspoken with my opinions. I was willing to give anything I was interested in a try, just to say I did it. I was braver than ever! Was this my mid-life crisis, or my "awakening" I kept hearing about from other women my age? Either way, I was having fun with it.

I started to dabble with makeup and hair styles. I wanted to change everything I ever once was and try new looks. I got a job working for a retail clothing company and found I loved fashion. The store I worked for offered an employee discount, so I updated my closet with some fancy digs. I felt like a runway model strutting around all day in my new outfits.

I was driving an hour to work, five days per week, and working in a big city full of people I didn't know. I felt like an animal let out of a cage. I was far from that little town, and away from everyone in it. I was free to be who I always wanted to be with nobody I knew watching my every step.

My self-confidence levels were over the top and people started to take notice. I would open that store and get everything rolling just as my job entailed. I was a "keyholder" and I was in charge. I opened the store and closed the store. I had a position of importance. I felt needed and appreciated. It felt amazing!

Since the store was owned by the same company I worked for prior, I could still online message her when I was doing my closing duties in the office. It felt comforting knowing we were still connected, even though it seemed like I was a whole other world away.

I would get the store closed around 10:00pm and drive back to town to meet up with her. She would get done around the same time as I would, and we'd stay out until they closed the bar down. The kids were at their dad's, so we didn't have anyone to go home to.

It was fun to have something to look forward to after being on my feet all day. I seriously walked ten miles a day in that store. And in high heels, I might add. I loved the shoes but hated what they were doing to my poor feet. But it was worth it. All that walking was complimenting me in other ways. I quickly lost ten pounds and was in the best shape ever. My skinny jeans fit me well, and I was, for once, proud of my body. I looked good! My boyfriend still treated me like shit, but I felt sexy anyway.

She would always get me to dance, and we'd shake our asses to the music playing and didn't care who was watching. We'd get up on the picnic tables outside and put on a show for everyone out there. The sex appeal we emitted when we were together was amazing. Everyone was turned on. We were wild and provocative. I felt like I was in an episode of 'Sex in the City'. I had the good job, nice clothes, great friends, and a smoking hot body. So why was I wasting my time on this idiot?

I became more adventurous in the bedroom, but not with just my boyfriend. When he would act like I didn't exist, it didn't bother me like it did before. I would just get the attention I needed from someone else. I would break up with him, then teach him a lesson.

It was amazing! I went through men like a bag of potato chips. It was easy. Men were easy. They gave me what I wanted, and I got to decide on whether to call them back again the next day.

I loved my newfound power. Now, we both had stories to tell. The drama of the night was the high we needed to get through the mundane crap that wasn't so glamorous at home. She would tell me about her latest escapade, and I would tell her about my love triangle that I had going on at the time. It seems my not so interested boyfriend became suddenly interested when I was with someone else. It was like a game of cat and mouse. I think he liked the "let's see if I can get her back" game, and I was loving the attention.

It was a sick and twisted way of life, but it was working for me. I was getting what I wanted, so I just went with it. But, like anything else, it didn't last. I loved my job and the confidence it gave me. He must have seen that too, because one day out of the blue, he needed me to manage the bar he owned. Funny, he never needed any help before when he was running around with his twenty-something bartenders everywhere. I knew what he was doing, but decided to ignore the huge red flag waving in front of my face and put my two weeks' notice in the next day.

I not only got a new position, but he bought a big diamond ring to put on my finger to sweeten the deal. Even though I had to put it on my own finger without a proposal, I told myself this is what I wanted and made the best of it. Things were changing for the better...or were they?

The engagement lasted exactly one year. I realized he had no intentions of marrying me. It just looked good having his fiancé managing his business. Even though I took the ring off my finger and moved out, he kept me on as manager. Which worked out for both of us.

I must have gone through an identity crisis there for a bit, because I became hooked on watching makeup tutorials and became attached to a certain brand. It was a MLM business. I had no experience but decided to sign up under one of my idols and try my hand at selling makeup. I was the "makeup lady", or so my online handle said. I would do live videos demonstrating the products and how to use them. I couldn't believe how bold I was in allowing myself to be so vulnerable in front of an audience, with my face up close in the camera. But I was doing it and was doing it well. I became well-known around the area. People would comment on seeing my videos and I felt like a movie star in that little town.

I would experiment with new looks and show them off while I bartended. All my friends turned into my guinea pigs and would come over and allow me to transform them into vamped up hookers. Hahaha!

I was doing their makeup for dates, weddings, Halloween parties, etc... I was having a blast! I now had a side gig too! I was making enough money to buy new products, and that was pretty much it. I wasn't doing as well as she was in her MLM business, but it was a start.

It's funny, because I remember when she first told me about her "oils", I honestly thought this woman is a tree hugging hippie freak. I never in my life, met anyone so earthy as she was. I too, loved nature and all God's creatures, but she took it to the next level.

She was a believer in holistic medicine and preached on

a regular basis, how our government was silently poisoning us with the products we were buying off the store shelves. Sure, she smoked cigarettes and drank rum, but that never came up in conversation, and I never thought anything of it. They had to have been her only vices in trying to live a pure and healthy life.

I learned shortly after our newly budding friendship that she did this side-gig in her spare time for extra money. But it really wasn't her "side-gig". It was her life's passion! She blew me away with her scientific knowledge and everything she knew about natural herbal remedies in helping with everyday ailments, and gladly passed on the magic of her "witchy" ways to me.

I would always laugh at her when she slathered her Abundance Blend all over me whenever we met up. She would always smell as if she bathed in it. I'd jump in her vehicle, and she would gag and roll the window down at my department store perfume and tell me it was poison.

She was that friend that would blow out my burning candles and inform me of their toxicity. She alerted me to the dangers of beauty products harboring silent, but deadly chemicals absorbed through the skin. I began to wonder how I ever made it to be the age that I was.

I grew up in a household of narcotics in the medicine cabinet and chemicals in the cupboard. Whatever was on sale at the grocery store, is what my mother brought home. I never knew any other way of life. This was all some new kind of voodoo to me. But I was intrigued by it.

Multi-Level Marketing is something I could never wrap my head around. Like most people, I thought it to be a "pyramid scheme" and never planned on making any real income from it. She, on the other hand, knew the assignment and figured out how to make it work for her.

Her love for Gary Young and his essential oils was almost cult-like in my eyes. I had never seen such passion displayed for a product and way of life. And it wasn't just her, everyone involved felt just as driven as she did in what they were doing.

Her gift of making people feel at ease around her, was like gold when it came to recruiting people to her team of oilers. She was a natural! She climbed that "pyramid" close enough to the top to where she was bringing in a decent amount of extra income every month. She called it residual income. It allowed her to live her independent life away from him. The longer I knew her, the more I started believing in her alternative lifestyle.

I started experimenting with essential oils and all natural products and became hooked. I really got into it and decided to give it a try. She signed me up and I was off and rolling. Literally. I'd make up roller bottles of essential oil blends that helped with dry scalp, acne, bug bites, period cramps, wrinkle prevention, etc. The list was endless!

I would make my own household products that I would use to clean my house and wash my clothes. I promoted them every chance I got. I signed up everyone I knew. I held classes one night per week and set up a booth at all the vendor shows I could, to exploit the chemical-free life I had found. I was an herbalist, or what others would call a witch.

Sure, it was a lot of extra work, but I was enjoying it, and people seemed interested in an alternative lifestyle. The extra income wasn't too bad either. I remember signing up eight people in just one month. I couldn't get enough of it. I wanted to learn everything I could on these amazing little bottles of gold. And who better to teach me than someone I trusted and admired? Her wishes of abundance were coming true. I felt blessed.

5

Things can only get worse

As children, we have no say in where we are placed and with whom we trust in caring for us. There is a lot of failure in this. Innocent children placed in violent situations. I will never understand it.

Although my parents never divorced, as hers did, I understood what a "broken" family consisted of. My family was broken, but we continued to live under the same roof. I would've loved getting a break from my mother every weekend, but it never worked out that way.

Her parents were high school sweethearts who split up, but as I heard it, her father never got the memo. He would randomly show up whenever her mother started seeing someone else and proceed to beat him up. I had already heard stories on what a violent man he was, back in the day. The bar regulars told me he was the local "tough guy" that would always end up in a fight wherever he hung out. He liked fast cars and fist fighting. Everyone respected him out of fear. You wanted to be on his good side, versus the alternative. So, people let him do pretty much what he wanted to do. Even the authorities.

She would tell me how relentless he was in making her mother's life a living hell, and how her mother had to move to Arizona just to get away from him.

Ahhhh...the good 'ole days. When a man could pretty much do whatever, he wanted to a woman, married to her, or not. Nobody stepped in to help this poor woman. Go figure. I still see him out and about every now and then. He never left town. I mean come on! When you're that famous, you never leave. Oh sure, he calmed down with age, but knowing what I know, I can still see violence in his eyes, that tells me he is still used to getting what he wants.

Anyway, back to my story. Her mother grew tired of his constant surprise visits and manipulation, so she left her old life behind and started her new life somewhere warm. It seems he didn't really care whether his children were in his life, or not. He was just set on teaching her mother a lesson by making her life as miserable as possible.

Funny how history repeats itself. It sounded like what my friend was currently going through with her own divorce. Only, I don't believe she had to deal with as much violence as her mother did. All her ex did was stalk her and belittled everything she accomplished without his permission.

I'm not sure of her mother's mental health at the time of the move, but with the constant bullying, I'm sure she was at her wits end. Turns out it wasn't all sunshine and roses in Arizona either. Her mother became addicted to drugs and started hanging out with friends that joined in the fun. It was the 80s after all and drugs were plentiful. Her mother began to live a free-spirited lifestyle. She was an eccentric that built her new adobe home from the ground up with her own hands. People around here called it whacko. Or that is what her ex wanted everyone to believe.

My friend was forced to live with relatives, while she finished high school. Because her father had moved on to someone else and had another family to take care of. Nice. I'm thinking that's when she met Mr. Wonderful. She told me of the teenage drama she endured while staying with extended family, who seemed to not want the responsibility. She was homeless on more than one occasion while attending high school. So naturally, she would run to her "knight in shining armor", that promised to take care of her. He became her "refuge". What a joke. Did she even have a choice? She was just trying to survive.

After she graduated, she attended a local Technical College, where she obtained an associate's degree in Tourism and Recreation. She took her degree and moved back to Arizona, where she worked as a Concierge for the Hilton Hotel. She was winning at life, but it seems her successful life in the sunshine state wasn't enough for her. She came back to marry her high school sweetheart and start a family right away. Barefoot and pregnant, just the way he liked her.

Don't get me wrong, she loved being a mother and put everything she had into it. She was an amazing mother to all three of her children, and him. She ran around taking care of everyone. Him, his dad, his brothers, on top of her children. Every woman's dream. Hillbilly heaven.

He had his own business but seemed to work only when he wanted to. When money got tight, she got a job. A second shift job that allowed her to homeschool her kids during the day. He wasn't crazy about the idea of her having a life outside of the home, but the money he happily took from her made it all worthwhile.

She did this for at least 13 years before she began to tire of it. He became lazy and didn't finish what he started. She told me of all the unfinished projects he would start around the house just to pacify her restlessness. But the yard ended up looking like a junkyard and her dream home never did get finished.

When she made the decision to move out, he acted like it was a conspiracy against him, even though she warned him repeatedly of the consequences of his lack of action. I don't think he could fathom the idea of her walking out the door. He relied on her loyalty and knew how much she loved him. He depended on her love of being a family and living in that house. He used it against her. Called her bluff and lost.

Her newfound freedom didn't bring the happiness she imagined. She would often cry because she missed her home. She wanted the fairytale, but his promises were never brought to life. He never apologized for any of it. Instead, he went out and found someone that looked just like her to take her place.

It wasn't a good decision on his part. She was mad as hell. But he thought it all to be a joke. He would sneak in to see her, behind his new girlfriends back, and lie to his new victim about the continuing relationship he had going with his ex-wife.

He played both sides so well. He was getting his cake and eating it too. He had an ex who was jealous of the replacement, and tried to steal his attention, while living with the "body double" who cleaned up after him and kept his bed warm. The fucker even went so far as to withhold child support from her.

He had his own flooring business and decided how much and when he got paid. He lied through his teeth about his wages. It's a good thing she was successful at both jobs she was maintaining. She found herself constantly in and out of the courtroom, just trying to get the bare minimum out of him. He even did the unthinkable and forged her name on the insurance check they received for a fire that started in the bathroom of their house. She was still half owner of the home. But he cashed that check and bought himself a new Mustang.

Meanwhile, she was fighting to make ends meet living without his financial support. I always thought she lived rent-free, since her father was her landlord. Then she told me that he charged her full price every month. Why would I expect anything else? What a dump. He let his daughter and grandsons live in that squirrel infested place, without so much as changing a lightbulb. She just couldn't catch a break. Not even from her own father.

She would tell me that her father thought she should go back home and stop the ridiculousness of their separation. He never had her back and would never stand up to her ex, even when he decided to break into her home, or talk his shit against her. Hell, they were even buddies who got together often and compared notes. Birds of a feather, flock together.

Now you see why I wanted to strangle him in chapter one? A real piece of work. He would invite himself over after she was already passed out from drinking and have his way with her. She would tell me when he did this, and I told her to file rape charges. She wouldn't. She didn't want to do that to her children.

Always about someone else, and never about her. She always put others first, knowing they put her last.

Her father was only one of her "let downs" in her life. One day she got a phone call from a friend of her mother's, that also lived in Arizona, telling her that her mother was strung out on drugs and having what she thought, was a mental breakdown. So, amidst the grueling divorce at hand, she flew to Arizona to pack up her mother, sell her house, and bring her back to town. She received no help from any other family members. What the fuck?

Just what she needed. Someone else to take care of. I'm not

going to go into all the nasty details, but to give you some idea of the severeness of this situation, just imagine getting a phone call in the middle of the night, from the local sheriff's department, stating that they found your mother crawling up the middle of main street, in her nightgown, causing a semi driver to slam on his brakes and stop dead in his tracks. Word gets around in a small town.

She would abruptly leave our nightly excursions on more than one occasion, to go and take care of her mother's messes. The embarrassment she was feeling must have been unbearable. But she was always there for her mother in her time of need. What a shame that it was never reciprocated. Especially when my friend really needed her mother during that time.

But instead of receiving gratitude for her good deeds, she would always receive backlash from her mother after incidences like this. Her mother would accuse my friend of being self-righteous and finger-pointing. She would accuse her of making things up, when told accounts of what happened. She was forced to perform random searches of her mother's home looking for drugs, and when she would find painkillers in the kitchen drawer, her mother would tell her that she had no right going through her home and would send elaborate text messages on wanting to end her life. Yet, when given the chance at therapy, would never admit she needed any help. And why would she? She had her daughter to care for her every need. She had her daughter to clean up all the messes she made in her life.

Bullying father and ex-husband, and a self-absorbed codependent mother. The cards were stacked against her.

I believe the stress and trauma my friend endured for nearly all her life, lay dormant inside and later manifested disease. I truly believe the people that were meant to love and care for her, became ingredients in her recipe for death. How much can one body and mind endure? I blame the three of them in taking turns at destroying her existence. I don't believe in karma, but I can't imagine their lives holding anything good after what they have done to her.

6

Friendly Fire

Remember that one house growing up, where all the kids hung out? You would walk in the door and trip over a sea of shoes, because everyone you knew was there.

She had a soul that I often compared to as an open door. I don't recall her ever locking the door. People would just open the door and holler out her name to see if she was home or not.

You would walk in and instantly feel warm and welcomed. I would describe her style as a "Boho Maximalist". It was never pristine and untouchable. Everything was well used and arranged in a relaxed, yet cozy configuration that made you feel at home. Just like her, everything she owned had a story. She was a sentimental being who held on to everything that was dear to her heart. The scent of essential oils and herbs, along with whatever was still on the stove from the night before, filled the rooms with a comforting aroma that reminded you of somewhere, but couldn't recall ever being.

She moved a couple times since that place, but still made everywhere she ended up feel as if she lived there forever. I have memories from all the places she lived and felt at home in all of them.

The last place she lived in, I was only in a handful of times, but everything remains as I remember it since she passed away. Her wish was to die at home, and her wish was granted. Even though she has left this earth, her spirit still lingers, and her children have left it looking as if she still lived there. I drive past at least once per week, and if I squint my eyes just right, I can still see her sitting on her porch.

I'll drop off a casserole for her boys whenever I can, and while there, I can still read the words written over the kitchen sink, "I am healed" in her handwriting on the window. It takes everything I have to refrain from bursting into tears at the broken promises she made to herself in trying to stay positive.

She is in every speck of dust settled on the floor. She is in every fingerprint still lingering on the refrigerator door handle. I don't want anything about her home to ever change, but my mind always wanders back to the apartment she lived in when I first met her.

I remember her enclosed front porch filled with plants, dream catchers, and dotted with art projects created by her boys. We spent many nights sipping our drinks while watching the traffic at the stop sign below. She lived in one of the buildings her father owned. It used to be a popular paint store in town and her grandparents lived upstairs for years. There was no longer a business downstairs, so we had the place pretty much all to ourselves.

She would often have people over, for a daytime get-together, or an after bar, and I remember it filled to the rim with a collection of people that I had never met before but would later come to know.

I was always amazed at the diversity among them. Some were exactly like her, earthy and peace-loving, while others were chaotic, and hard to be around. I found myself pondering what the connection was between them and how they came to be friends. Whatever it was, she welcomed them, just as she welcomed me into her home, so I never gave it too much thought.

She was a natural at hosting a party. She would always be at ease and spend her time interacting with everyone instead of stressing over the mess in the kitchen. She didn't give a shit if her place had a lived-in look. Life had more meaning to her than a sink full of dirty dishes. She prioritized what was important to her and loved opening her home up to people that she cared about.

At the time, I just felt as one of the many sheep that flocked to her side, but as time went by, I realized there was something different about our connection. I don't know how to describe it. We just knew how the other was feeling, or what they were thinking, despite what they were showing others out in the public eye. We would always give each other that secret look, that told each other how we really felt at the time.

She was never one to discriminate against religion, sex, money, relationship status, gender, politics, or the color of skin. If she liked you, she liked you and that was that. But if you purposely offended her, trying to trigger a response, well...you got one. She wasn't someone you could easily upset, but when you did, look out! The Scorpio in her came out and her words cut you like a razorblade deep to your core. She was very "wordy" and knew all the right ones to say when needed. I loved that about her, because I too had learned the power of words. I learned that words could do way more lasting damage than physical violence. You just had to choose the right ones when the damage needed to be done. If she told you off, you probably deserved it, and you would never forget it.

She was a people person who loved being involved in any local event that was going on. Anywhere there was live music and dancing, is where she longed to be. She always like the way I listened to the lyrics and shared what they were. She just loved the beat and would drag me out onto the dance floor. You didn't dare resist, or she would just start dancing with you right where you stood. I lived some of the best times of my life with her.

Sometimes another friend would join us in our adventures, and we would dominate that place. If the three of us were out, then you knew you were in for a good time. We'd turn them on and leave them thinking they did something wrong. A bunch of "dick teasers". We were having so much fun together, we didn't want some man ruining it for us. Three jilted women on a mission to get even with the world that robbed us of our happiness.

As long as everyone was having fun, there were no problems. But, as in every group, there is always one or two that like to stir shit up. The "whisperers" who spew their mindless gossip as soon as your back was turned.

There were only two amongst us that would smile as your friend when confronted face-to-face with you, and as soon as you left the room, had nothing good to say about you. I knew who they were. That's why I never had a desire to be intimate with them, outside of our group events. Sometimes I would even make up an excuse to leave myself out of the picture all together if I heard they were going to tag along.

I never knew the reason for such animosity between us. I don't recall ever offending them in any way. I just seen it as jealousy. They wanted her all to themselves, and I could see through their false friendships. There for a while, the drama was endless. I felt physically ill just trying to fake a smile when I was in the same room with them. I only put myself through it for her sake. I didn't want to lose her friendship, but something seemed different about her whenever they were around. "Mean girls" never had a place in my life. I wasn't one to be bullied into anything, so I started new friendships with other people, and decided I wasn't going to be part of their group.

It broke my heart to see a riff in our relationship, but I knew deep in my heart that our true friendship would survive. I wasn't going to be the one to give her any ultimatums, so I decided to wait it out and hope for the best.

What was sad about all of this was it occurred in the last year of her life. I missed out on some precious moments because of my defiance and unyielding resistance to their charms. As I said before, "Birds of a feather flock together", and I wasn't going to be part of that murder of crows. In doing so, our friendship became colder and more distant. I missed being with her, but we continued to keep in contact through private messaging and sharing funny memes to each other. It just wasn't the same as before, and they loved that. Their side-eyed smirks revealed their secret win to get her all to themselves. But they would never have what we had...ever.

I went about my life as if I was fine in all of it. I kept busy and documented everything I did with my new acquaintances on Facebook and Instagram. I don't know what was going through her mind when she would see them, because she never brought it up. She was doing her own thing too. There were days though that I could tell by her deep sighs that it did bother her. Especially when we would get together for a drink and she was bartending.

That's right...she ended up working at the bar my ex owned. I hired her, because she ended up leaving that factory job, and living strictly off her residual income she was making from her essential oil gig. It was only a couple days per week, and a little extra money couldn't hurt, so I asked her, and she thought it would be fun. It was perfect. I needed a friendly face behind the bar that people enjoyed being around and she excelled at it, as I knew she would.

Her ex wasn't as ecstatic as she was, but who cared what he thought? I sure didn't. She had a regular following that would come in knowing she was behind the bar, and she always made sure she left it in tiptop shape for me the next morning. She was one of the most thorough and hardworking employees I ever hired.

She never took advantage of our friendship and always showed respect towards me and accepted any suggestions I made when wearing my "manager" pants. She would openly give her opinions on how she would do things, but knew when to let it go, if she knew I wasn't going to budge on anything I decided to do. She let me do it my way, even though she went to school for the very thing I was doing and ran a financially successful business of her own.

I will always admire her for that. I miss her comradery, and I miss her always in my corner when it came to my job. She knew how hard it was to work for my ex. He would cross the line between work and play often, and she would tell him to knock it off and leave me alone. She never encouraged me to get back with him, knowing how convenient it would have been with me already running his business. She knew what I went through with him, and she knew I was finished with that overworked fantasy. Everything was just as it should be, and I didn't want to change a thing. I just wished we were as close as we once were.

7

Soul Mates

Earlier, I told of experimenting with new experiences. Having a history of being a good catholic girl, I always thought of sex as either sinful, or just one more thing that I was expected to do as a woman.

I was raised never to taste from the forbidden fruit, unless it was within marriage. When I lost my virginity to the boy next door, I honestly thought we were going to be forever. I was absolutely crushed when I learned different. So, I ended up marrying the second man I ever slept with, and that was the first biggest mistake of my life. After our divorce, I decided that rule was out the window, and I slept around with three different men that I had no intention of ever marrying.

Then I met husband number two while working as a cashier at the local grocery store. He was a local police officer, and once again, I found myself trying to be something I wasn't. The perfect little woman. It lasted around fourteen years, so I patted myself on the back for putting in more effort than the first.

So, as a recently TWICE divorced woman, I was no longer interested in doing all the "right" things that I was once told to do. Fuck that. I was in my "men" era. I was trying them on as if they were new outfits. The only problem was, instead of putting them in my closet, I couldn't take them off fast enough.

I always loved the idea of having a man in my life and I don't recall ever being without one. Even though I had the less than desirable situation going on with Mr. Wonderful, I still considered it "having a man" in my life. Ridiculous.

My friend was having the same results as I was, only she wanted to keep them, even though she couldn't make herself do it. I'm glad for it. Her choice in men was worse than mine. The things she would disclose the next day were the very reasons I would completely stop having sex.

Just like the popular phrase these days, "fuck around and find out", she did. She knew who he was from earlier encounters but never imagined him playing a leading role in her life. News flash...the person you have been looking for your whole life, might very well be right under your nose.

He wasn't the most romantic man, and yet he was. He was rough and callous on the outside, yet soft and gentle on the inside. He had the look she liked, and believe it or not, his laugh was just as infectious as hers. You should have heard the two of them out together. It was hilarious! She'd say something and he would roar. Literally. Then he would do or say something that made her collapse into a convulsion of laughter. It made you want to laugh, even though you didn't know what in the hell they were laughing at.

He became a regular at her place, and even the kids were getting to know him. Everything seemed great. She finally had her man that she was craving and started to feel safe and loved. She belonged to someone, and that is all she ever wanted.

I'd like to say her prayers were answered, but that doesn't happen to women like us. With every joy came great pain. Even though the huge red flag was waving in her face, in her search for contentment, she decided to turn the other way and ignore the signs. He was everything she was looking for and he was right under her nose this whole time. Burley, kind, funny, spontaneous, and a raging alcoholic.

In the beginning, they were having too much fun unraveling their entangled lives, to be bothered with complicated details. But the pitfalls were inevitable.

Apparently, the after bars became a little more than she wanted to deal with. He would get to her place and suddenly become jealous of every man she smiled at, spoke to, or dated in the past. He didn't like her bartending and was under the impression that all bartenders fucked around. But he was wrong. Since day one of their meeting each other, she remained faithful until the end.

She was at a loss on what to do with him. Although he was never violent with her, she feared his behavior around her kids. The constant bickering and wild accusations had to come to a stop. After more than one heart-to-heart conversation, and many ultimatums, he decided to go to rehab. I remember the day he left, and thinking to myself, how desperately in love he was to do something as profound as that. The ultimate sacrifice on his part. If only it had turned out better than it did.

He went to rehab and successfully sobered up. He said it was hell, and I believed him. There, for a while, he would come in and drink soda. Then after a while, he would just stay home altogether. I saw it as a successful decision on his part, but his feelings of unworthiness and shame, overran any triumphant gains he was making, and he fell right back into his personal hell.

She started to find bottles of booze stuck in every nook and corner of the house while cleaning. Hidden away, for she didn't even know how long. The trust that they once had was eroding away at an alarming rate.

Now, he was sure she was unfaithful to him, because he let

her down. The arguments became a reason for him to drink even more than before, and she had no other choice but to kick him out of her house.

It broke her heart to be so severe, but I feel she did it to save him. She honestly thought that their relationship was stronger than his urge to drink.

In locking her door, he ended up staying with other people. Including his ex-girlfriends and ex-wife. Apparently, he was hanging out with them quite frequently. Now that she had proof of his unfaithfulness, she couldn't justify taking him back into her life. The love of her life became another burden for her to carry.

Oh sure, she'd try and pretend that it was something she could get over, but I knew it was breaking her heart. They spent two years together and experienced every high and low imaginable. You just don't "get over" something as profound as what they had.

Along with the heavy drinking, rumor had it that there were other addictions happening too. He was too far gone to reach and the hope of rekindling their connection disappeared forever. She needed him more than he will ever know.

Love is hard. Love is painful. But you know what's worse? Finding out that you have cancer. As if a broken heart wasn't bad enough, let's add a rare and aggressive terminal illness to her plate.

I remember her taking a river rafting trip with some friends and coming home without her voice. She said she fell in the river and almost drowned. I wonder why God decided to save her? She could have just drowned and be spared the suffering awaiting her.

She thought maybe swallowing all that water might have done something to her throat, so she ended up going to a doctor as soon as she got back from her trip.

I can't remember the exact day in July, but I remember the look on her face as she was telling me her prognosis... two months. There's no way. How can someone only live two months after the first symptoms just started?

She later found out that the reason she was having difficulty swallowing and speaking, was because there was a tumor pressing on her windpipe. She was diagnosed with Anaplastic Thyroid Cancer. Look it up. One of the most aggressive cancers a person can be diagnosed with, with a survivorship phase of only five to six months.

They gave her two, which I knew in my heart of hearts, wasn't going to be the case. She was a fighter. I will elaborate on this later. For now, the diagnosis was enough for the love of her life to step to the plate and be strong for her. She was going to need a shoulder to cry on, and who better than with someone as familiar with pain as he was.

They decided to put their bitterness aside and enjoy each other's company while they could. He tried his damnedest to be the strong and steady man she needed at the time, but his addiction got the best of them both.

Have you ever had one of those dreams, where you are drowning, and you awake with such violence that you sit straight up in bed gasping for air? That was her life. She was doing her best to stay positive and afloat in the angry waters she was pushed into. She had to stay focused on surviving each day, and he ended up being the large boulder tied to the rope around her neck. She tried...she really did. She secretly hoped along her journey that he would choose her, in her time of need, but it didn't end up that way. It ended up way worse.

I was in our local thrift store that morning when I got the call. I almost dropped the phone when she told me the news..." he's dead". He had called her minutes before, begging her to take him back. She could tell he was drunk and high on something other than alcohol. Little did she realize that it would be his last words to her. She was upset, and told him she wasn't going to talk to him in the state he was in. When she hung up, so did he. He ended his life by hitting a cement support under an overpass. He was dead on arrival. We will never know if he just lost control, or if it was intentional.

The nightmare keeps getting worse. How is one to stay positive during all this? There is no earthly way. The guilt that she carried from that day forward, was just another nail in her coffin. She lost her soulmate. The one she wanted to be with during her numbered days. In the days to follow, she found out he was once again living with his ex-wife, and she was planning his wake and funeral along with his family.

My friend was not invited, or welcomed to the ceremony, but she showed up anyway. She showed up with her own memorabilia, and collection of photos for her own memory board. She was a class act, and kept her composure during the whole thing, but I could see the betrayal in her eyes.

Her love for him was treated like a dirty little secret that no one dared to mention throughout that day. People passed right by her on the way to the receiving line filled with his family and ex-wife. The tension was almost unbearable, but she stayed until the bitter end. The courage and strength that woman had, was unmatched by anyone I have ever known. I couldn't have been prouder, yet heartbroken for her at the same time.

Her journey had already lasted 6 months longer than it was supposed to. She was never going to let cancer end her in just two months. Her journey was only half done, and he was there for most of the beginning of her fight. Even though they were having problems, she still knew he was there if she ever needed him. He was her friend, and he did love her.

8

The Party Never Stops

What does one do when they are faced with their own mortality? Do you surrender and lie down, and never again get out of bed? Or do you go on like no one ever told you that you only had two months to live? That your children would live out their young adult lives without you there.

I always pondered the motive behind doctors finding it necessary to give you your "expiration date"? Was it so that you could plan your exit? Or was it to put you in such a panic, that you would do anything to stay alive? And by that, I mean be willing to be a human guinea pig and let them perform their trials with all kinds of "groundbreaking" drugs and experiments on you, in the hopes that they might cure you of your eminent doom.

I think if given the same situation as she was given, I would have chosen the latter of the two choices out of panic. I was one of those fools who held on to the belief that modern medicine wanted nothing but the best outcome for you. But that was until I'd seen firsthand how important you really are to them. Money plays a big part in cancer treatment. It's as if the medical industry depends on your illness in order to benefit from it. Well people do not make them any money and insurance companies are not going to willingly pay for something that works in keeping you healthy. They want something that will take a long and painful amount of time and end up costing you more than you will ever be able to pay back. You die in financial ruin as a statistic they add to their collected scientific data.

If she only had two months to live then why would they try to talk her into doing chemotherapy? Hmmm... in other words, we know you are dying, but that doesn't mean you still can't make us rich. They presented her with the option of spending her last two months on this earth so deathly ill, that she would wish she was dead, and to top that off, do it completely bald.

This woman had the most beautiful hair that I had ever seen on a woman's head. She always wore it long with layers that would fall gently into place without effort. I was so jealous. My hair had to be tamed with sprays and gel, along with a hot curling iron that fried my ends.

I loved how her hair perfectly framed her beautiful face. Funny thing though, she was always self-conscience of her forehead. I didn't think it too large and would try and pull her hair back or put it up in an updo, but she said too much forehead was showing and would wear it down. It's funny how we all have our own insecurities about our bodies and how we look, and the thought of losing all her hair was not an option for her. Why can't modern medicine come up with a cancer cocktail that doesn't make you lose all your hair? It's bad enough that you're nauseous, tired, and weak...but bald too? And not just the hair on your head. You lose ALL or your hair. All your body hair, your eyebrows, and sometimes eyelashes too.

A woman that is faced with the fate of a short time to live, knows that she isn't going to live long enough to grow any of it back. She didn't want to die bald. I wonder if she was given a guarantee of being cancer-free after her chemo, if she would have done it differently than she did. But as vain as it sounds, she didn't want to die ugly. But then again, no one does.

I remember my father in the last stages of his life. He too died of cancer and was a bald skeleton of a man lying in his hospital bed in the end. I can't get the image out of my head. I'm sure she didn't want her boys to remember her that way either.

Faced with a lack of money, and lack of time, she did what she could on her own to save her own life. As I mentioned earlier, she was very intelligent and began to research her options. Which was frowned upon by the medical world. Since she refused their toxic offer, she was snubbed by the specialists that were supposed to help in keeping her alive.

They would warn her on all the negative side effects of her holistic approach. Which was so fucking ironic, since the alternative given her, could give her long term side effects, or kill her. They looked at her as if she lost her mind, on choosing to live a "quality" remainder of her life.

She had questions that they would no longer answer. They wrote her off and stopped referring her to organ specialists. Even her own oncologist ignored her phone calls and acted as if she was already dead. Apparently, people that value their life experience, and question any decision made by any doctor, is frowned upon. You are seen as the enemy for fighting for your life. While choosing a gentler approach to health, she closed the door on modern medicine. They heard her knocking but refused to open the door. Fucking assholes.

Even though she opted out of chemo, her holistic methods were still going to hit her hard in the pocketbook. The Immunotherapy, IV-Therapy (vitamin C infusions), Infrared light therapy sessions, special diet including all organic foods, and alternative medications that hadn't been approved by the FDA, none of it was covered by her insurance. That's where I came in. There were so many people who wanted to help, so I gave them a platform to do it. With the help of some very determined friends, we put on a fundraiser that in the end, raised $25,000 to help her in her quest.

I remember her fear in not living long enough to see the day, when I told her we couldn't plan until September 17th. Her diagnosis and prognosis were just shy of two months earlier. That poor woman. I cannot fathom the nightmare living within her mind, all the while remaining positive and uplifting for the public eye and her kids. Why do good people suffer the most in this world?

I assured her that she would not die before her day, and would attend, strong as ever. People bought the T-shirts, wristbands, and the donation jars were jammed full of cash. People all over the county donated items for silent auction and customers at the tavern where we worked, gladly volunteered in gathering these items. The event took up two spaces, and both were filled with everyone wanting to help in her fight. I was so humbled. She was blessed in seeing with her own eyes, all the people she touched during her lifetime, that wanted to give back. The love that poured out of everyone that day was unbelievable. We were all exhausted from our efforts, but they paid off. Now she had some funds to start her on her fight for her life. She had already beat the odds she was given and was gifted the strength and stamina to take it to the next level. She was born a fighter and had been training all her life for this fight. Nobody was going to tell her to lie down and submit to anything she did not see as moral or vital.

She had a circle that supplied all the information she needed, and how to get it. Her years as a certified spiritual healer and aromatherapist came into the spotlight. And all of her "earthy" comrades came to the rescue. Her days became diligently scheduled routines I like to compare to as a holistic boot camp. She couldn't stop and had to keep up. Her days became filled with fasting, drinking herbal concoctions, all-natural medications, juicing, sound therapy using low-frequency vibrations, meditation, spiritual enlightenment, reading, exercise, vitamin infusions, light therapy, etc..., and still found time to have some fun.

She would go to as many concerts as she could and took weekend trips with her friends and family. She tried to fit in every lasting memory her grueling schedule would allow. She had the energy of ten people! I was in awe of her stamina and grit. The phrase became "Tracy Strong", and it still holds true today. I have yet to meet anyone stronger. To think she did all that while sick and still had a smile and a laugh left inside of her, was unfathomable to me. It made me even sadder knowing how much she wanted to live. She deserved to live.

She never gave up the fight, and moreover, she would still show up for all her shifts at the bar. I can count on one hand the nights she had to find a replacement in the last two years of her fight. She relied on the normalcy of bartending a few nights per week and I'm sure the extra money was also a plus.

To this day, I experience guilt every time I think I need a day off, because of her dedication to her job. What do I need a day off for? I am lucky to have a job and feel healthy enough to do it. Seriously...ugh! I have grown callous when it comes to people whining about their jobs. I don't want to hear it!

I still have the text message of her apologizing for having to give up her shift because she was having trouble keeping her balance while on her feet. She showed up sick, dizzy, tired, depressed, and now she couldn't do her job, which told me she was on the decline. She wasn't going to give up, she just didn't want to do her job poorly. To this day I wish I could find another employee with such dedication.

9

WHY?

I believe in a heaven; and I believe in a hell. I also believe that both can be experienced here on earth. They say bad things happen in groups of three. Then why did they seem to keep coming one right after another with her?

She refused chemo, but did opt for the surgery to remove part of her thyroid. In doing so, she lost what was left of her voice. Her vocal cords were damaged during the procedure. Little did I know at the time, I would never again hear that glorious laugh of hers. Thank God I have videos with sound to remind me.

They assured her that her situation was temporary, and that her vocal cords would heal in time. But they didn't. So, she was put on a waiting list for a collagen injection to help plump up her damaged vocal cord. After 6 months of waiting, still with no voice, the day finally arrived. I remember her being so excited to be able to talk again and I was excited for her. Everything went well that day and they sent her home with high hopes.

Finally, a little slice of heaven in her daily hell. But it didn't last long. While recovering at home, she woke up one morning and couldn't breathe. They rushed her to the hospital and found that she had a rare allergic reaction to the injection and ended up having to have an emergency tracheotomy to open her airway. And what's worse, they did the procedure while she was awake!

Not only did she not have a voice, but she couldn't clear her throat, or cough. She had to relearn how to eat, drink, and get used to breathing out of the tube protruding from her neck!

She sent me a selfie of her lying in her hospital bed after the procedure. It was heartbreaking. The pain in her eyes was unbearable. Why? If this was her penance, my question was "what sins did she ever commit in her life to deserve this"? Where was the fucking karma everyone swears by? Her positivity levels plummeted, and why wouldn't they? Another stumbling block. What was supposed to be a routine procedure with a 75% success rate, now ended in worse than just losing her voice.

She struggled with the trach for months. It oozed and gurgled while she talked. She was constantly touching it to make sure it wasn't leaking, and in doing so it became sore and painful. But through it all, she still came to work and tried her best to live as normal a life she could. People knew it bothered her but chose to look the other way and never brought it up in conversation. We were just happy she chose to show up for us.

With everything she had already been through, you would think she would catch a break. But she didn't. Not even a sliver of light was offered in her nightmare of darkness. She endured the loss of her dear friend and lover in the months to follow and ended up going through the remainder of her fight alone.

When she was offered another try at an injection to get her voice back, she declined, and the trach came out. She just accepted the fact that she would never get her voice back. Even though that was a hard pill to swallow, I could tell she was relieved that this chapter of her life was over.

Meanwhile, her scans looked hopeful. All her diligent work in trying to stay alive was paying off. Some of the nodules that were originally present during her first scan had disappeared, while others popped up elsewhere. She was defying the odds, and already lived six months longer than the sentence given her. Her nine months of one thing after another didn't sway her from trying to stay in a positive mindset. I don't think anyone else could have done it.

I believe some of us suffer as children to prepare us for what is in store for us in our adulthood. To "toughen us up". From what she told me about her childhood, she was well prepared. Sure, we all have had our share of bad weather, but why does the rain cloud hover over certain people throughout their whole lives? What was their purpose in life? To suffer endlessly? What does that teach those of us looking on? Is it to teach us humility, and gratitude?

At some point we all bitch about the little mishaps that come and go in our lives. It's just natural. But now when listening, I compare the "problem" at hand to her life. I know I shouldn't do that, because every person has their own history and story to tell. But seriously, I cannot listen to somebody whine about how they don't get any help cleaning the house, or how *he doesn't think I'm sexy anymore*, when she went through so much during her short life. You don't have a problem! Figure it out!

I sometimes try to recall the conversations that took place before all hell broke loose. Back when we didn't give a shit about what happened in our lives because we were having too much fun. I can only come up with conversations about the men that refused to give us what we wanted, and freedom. We were tired of being told what to do, and how we should do it. Our whole lives were dictated by someone else's rules. We obeyed our parents. We obeyed our husbands. We worked hard and went above and beyond what was expected of us as wives and mothers.

And for what? Where was the reward?

We made a pact to never be submissive to anyone, or anything ever again. We were never to be chained to anything that didn't bring us peace and happiness. She carried out her promise until the end. She never submitted to the opinions of others in what she should be doing to fight her cancer. She did it her way, and it was working. Other than the scar on her neck, she looked great. She was maintaining her weight. Her face glowed with health. Her skin looked better than ever. Her hair was silky and shiny. She had the energy of ten women. She made the time to get together with friends and experience life. She was going to concerts, getting tattoos, traveling with her boys, attending parties, touring places that she always wanted to see. She was experimenting with new foods and learning about nutrition. She would read numerous books and reach out to different groups with questions and was always given the answers she was searching for. She didn't stop. I often wondered if she ever slept. People were drawn to her and wanted to be near her. She was a living example of how you should live life. She wanted to thoroughly use it up and soak in everything she could. She deserved to live. She was a force that would never happen again. Her energy was unmatched by anyone I have ever and will ever know in my lifetime.

Her dream was to survive and publish a book on how she did it. She wanted to give others hope. To teach them how to overcome their fears of thinking outside of the box and to not trust in everything the medical community had to offer in keeping them alive.

Her kindness spilled out onto everyone around her. Even though her life may have seemed hopeless; she gave you the strength to carry on in your own life. She was my strength when I would feel sorry for myself about some dumb thing that was going on. All I had to do was follow her lead on how to keep marching on and never quit.

Her hopes in kicking cancer's ass were heightened by a clinic in Tijuana, that specialized in Integrative Cancer Treatments, but were not supported, or covered by her insurance. Go figure. But because of everyone's continued generosity and a lot of sacrifice on her part, she raised enough money to make the trip. It had been one year since we had the first fundraiser for her. She had already lived one year longer than she was expected to without conventional medicine, or procedures.

She got her passport and made the trip with her youngest son. I felt a surge of hope when she left. She was still strong, and seemed healthy, so I was sure the treatments were going to be the added force against the fight going on inside of her. The trip was also a much-needed break in her routine. She needed to get away and go somewhere warm and soothing to her soul.

She always did love the ocean, and her trips were mostly to destinations near, or right on the water. Being in another country never bothered her. She embraced other cultures and thoroughly soaked everything around her up. She was not an all-inclusive resort kind of person. She wanted to be where the locals were, and experience the food, music, and the local atmosphere just as they did.

Tijuana welcomed her with open arms. The doctors and nurses were not only nurturing but extended their hospitality way beyond their clinical appointments. Her doctor would drop off his kids at school and pick her and her son up every morning and drive them to the clinic. He invited them out to the local restaurants and allowed them to experience Tijuana as he did. She spent eight days there, receiving NK and LAK cells infusion/immunotherapy treatments, along with her other IV Therapies and Infrared light therapy treatments. Everything was paid for out of donations and money out of her pocket. I found out that there were those that speculated that she used her donated money to flip the bill for her adult son that accompanied her. She found it necessary to reassure everyone on her Facebook page that he was paying his own way to accompany her. Ridiculous! I hope the people that came out of the woodwork only to cause additional chaos in her life, will one day get the karma that they deserve in theirs. If there is such a thing. Unbelievable! She later found out that the people complaining hadn't even donated a dime to her cause. They only wanted to stir the "shit pot".

Nonetheless, her hope was renewed, and her positivity levels were restored. She had gone from worrying that she wouldn't live two months to see the day of her fundraiser, and lying in a hospital bed after her tracheotomy, with all hope crushed, to one year later feeling unstoppable. She was a miracle happening right before our eyes. She started to relax and allow herself to feel healthy again. She was talking again, but it was more like a hoarse whisper. You had to pay close attention to what she was saying because she struggled to talk. That seemed to be the only setback for the next six months. She would live to see another birthday, Thanksgiving, Christmas, and New Year's Day. Everything was right with the world.

10
The Chosen Few

I would give anything to relive those late nights in my shitty little apartment, feasting on frozen corndogs while stalking people on Facebook with my partner in crime. I only lived one block away from our favorite hangout, so sometimes she would end up there after last call to sober off a bit before going home. We worked second-shift, so there was plenty of time to sleep in the next day. Life was good. I just didn't realize how good it really was, at the time.

Friends are a common need we all share in life. It seems the older I get, I find that I only need at least one, or two close friends that I can reach out to. Although, I enjoy people, I'm not the kind of person to surround herself with people just so I can say I have a bunch of friends. I have always been kind of a loner. We weren't allowed friends for the longest time when growing up, so it is something I learned to do without. Even though I've been known to go out and party it up, my preference has always been to stay home. I don't need a lot of people in my life. I meet numerous people every day in my line of work, so I am happiest when I'm alone, or with one or two close friends in an intimate gathering.

I know there's probably some of you out there that have talked yourself out of needing any friends, or a social life, and I say bullshit! You need your people. Like I said, you don't need many. Good friends are more precious than gold. Friends are the family we choose to spend our lives with.

The sad truth is that we have no control where and with whom we are placed at birth. We are at the mercy of what, or whomever oversees our universe, and I sometimes find it hard to believe in a God for this very reason. How can anyone, or anything all knowing, place a helpless and dependent infant in the arms of a narcissist, a murderer, or a physically or mentally abusive parent?

Even children born into war zones and poverty, can feel safe if they are loved and nurtured, no matter what's going on around them. Home is where you should feel at peace. You can't escape the chaos. It is everywhere. No matter where you live it will find you and we all need refuge from this world, and home is our little piece of heaven where we can feel safe.

Laura Ingalls Wilder once wrote, *"there is no comfort anywhere for anyone who dreads to go home."* This quote lives in my mind because I've been there many, many times. I remember walking home from school as a little girl not wanting to go in that house, because I knew what I was going to be met with. It's a horrible place to be. Where do you go if you can't go home? It is hell on earth.

There are those who claim that we all start out the same in life. But you and I know that isn't the case. The only time we are ever the same, is when we all take our first breath. After that, the situations are different for everybody, and it is up to us to survive in this world by any way we learn how. And some don't survive. But others adapt and they overcome their terrible situations until they can make their own choices in life.

As adults, we begin to embrace our freedom and start to create our own home. We filled it up with people of our choice. We seek out people that calm us, inspire us, and maybe have similar likes and interests. They make us laugh and help us forget about our troubles for a fleeting moment. We look forward to being with them. They are handpicked by us and become our new home, or family away from home.

As we grow, our needs change, and sometimes, so do our friends. The friends we had in childhood may differ from the friends we choose as adults. Our attachments come and go with every new job, or move, but we continue to seek them out, because they are necessary for our survival and mental health. It's so important to find someone that gets you. Someone you can be yourself with, and if we are lucky enough, we find that friend in our life partner, husband, or wife. But that is rare. Because for most of us that isn't the situation.

We need our girl trips. We need a day golfing with the guys. We need to hang with our people. Our tribe that we meticulously picked out of the billions of people on this Earth just for us. We introduce them to our family, and we tell them our darkest secrets because there is a trust like no other. They sometimes become closer than our family. And over time, they become the family that we've always wanted but never had.

It took me forty plus years to figure this out. I thought I could go throughout life without close friendships and just devote all my time and energy to my husband and my kids. Boy...was I wrong. We all need a break. If I would have had a social life outside of my daily routine, I might not have gotten a divorce the second time around.

Women need other women. We need to gather and vent to each other. We find our strength when we come together. We learn that we are not alone and share a common bond. We get our advice and learn from each other. We laugh until we cry at the very things that consume us. Marriage is a two-way street. But I was the one, who allowed both husbands to control me and take away my social life. When you give away your power, you are half to blame for your own demise.

After my second divorce, I felt isolated and vulnerable. I had no one to talk to or turn to for advice. I didn't have another woman in my life who found herself struggling as I was. I would go home at the end of a long workday and dwell on all my problems until it was time for bed, wake up the next day, and do it all over again. I was miserable.

The day she first spoke to me outside on our smoke-break was the greatest turning point of my life. She didn't have to initiate conversation. She could have easily just finished her cigarette and went quietly back inside. But she didn't. I don't know if she recognized the familiar panic in my eyes or empathized with the weariness and fatigue, either way, I am grateful for her kindness. I made a new friend that day. A friend that became my family. A friend who let me be myself and laughed with me at my mistakes. A friend who didn't judge me when I got fucked up in life with all the wrong men. Who opened my eyes to all my capabilities and taught me to love myself and all my imperfections. I began to see myself through her eyes.

Surround yourself with people who honestly love you. Why are you friends with someone who makes you feel so uncomfortable. Stop faking friendships! Stop forcing friendships because of popularity, or financial status. Friendships come from the heart. It's a feeling you just have by being around them. Find your people! Find people that you can be yourself with. Even one special person in your life can make it so much better.

I found someone who knows how crazy my family can be. She's the one who knows how mean my mother can be and how toxic my ex really is. The one who knows how much I miss being in love but will never be less for anyone ever again. She knows how picky I am, this time around. She's the one who knows how much I love my kids and how I would die for any of them. Who knows how strong I can be when needed and how soft I really am. The one who knows what scares me the most. The one that knows what pisses me off and makes me want to cry... even if I don't.

I love that she knows me better than I have allowed anyone in this entire world to know me, and now I'm losing her to something I cannot see. I will never have another person like her the world, and I don't want one. I want her. I want her to live for my own selfish reasons. I need *her* as a friend. The world has become colder and there's nothing I can find in which to comfort myself. I believe I will silently shiver for the remainder of my days.

My only wish is that when I leave this earth, I will see her at the end of my journey, walking towards me with open arms, bathed in sunshine. Snort laughing at the things she's seen me do since she left. Greeting me with her sweet voice, "Hi hooker. I missed you."

11

Even Warriors Die

Just in case nobody ever told you, it doesn't matter how strong you are in life, because one day you too will fall away and leave this earth. When that time comes, you will be put into the ground, or scattered across the earth, never to be seen again. Over time, people will forget who you were and what you stood for and will never speak your name as they once did. Your existence will be forgotten sooner than you realize, and life will go on without you.

What a horrible reality. I may have dramatized a little, but the truth is that life is for the living. As cruel as it sounds, it is fact. Therefore, it is our job to keep their memory alive. It is our job to speak the names of those that have passed and share their story.

I still have the text message she sent, telling me she had to stop working at the bar. This woman rarely missed a shift. She loved her job, but now she was having a hard time keeping her balance and remembering what people ordered to drink. It seemed to all happen overnight. She explained how they wanted to do a scan on her brain and how she was terrified of the results.

Just days after she sent that message, she started having trouble texting anything at all. She was having vision problems, and her motor skills weren't cooperating. Little did I know in less than a month she would be gone.

I visited her two weeks before her rapid decline. She wanted some help cleaning up her front porch, where she enjoyed hanging out every chance she got. I rearranged her outdoor furniture and swept all the wet leaves from last autumn out of the corners and we sat and enjoyed the sounds of summer. The robins nesting in the trees with their new families, sounded like a winged chorus. The low hum of a lawnmower in the distance mixed with the sound of laughing children at play, it all made me want to cry. I could tell as she looked off into the distance, that she heard everything I was hearing, and savoring every waking moment of it all.

If I could choose the season of my death, it would never be summer. Who wants to leave when everything is buzzing with life. The smell of freshly mowed grass, and the sound of clumsy bumble bees floating from one bloom to another. The flicker of fireflies as evening falls, and gentle warm breezes that kiss your face and remind you how grateful you are to be alive. It would be horrible! I would always choose the dead of winter. When everything sleeps and there are no sounds to be heard other than the quiet snowflakes falling to the ground.

She slipped into the house and came back with something in her hand. She never talked to me about dying. She never mentioned it in our tete-a tetes. She always confirmed how she wasn't ready to leave and wouldn't be for a very long time. So, I was startled when she handed me a small Ziploc bag and watched me open it. Inside were two rings. One, I could tell was vintage, and the other was newer, but just as beautiful. There was also a handwritten note telling me the vintage ring belonged to her aunt, and how she thought the other, was just pretty. She wrote how she knew they would be loved and cherished by me and thanked me for watching over her children. It ended with "til we meet again and shake it on heaven's dance floor".

I just stared at her in disbelief. Was this the same woman who refused to even say the word *cancer*? It was her way of telling me, what I'm guessing, she had known for a while now. She was dying. How was I going to get through this?

Shortly after that day, she called to ask me to take her to the local Walmart Optical, so that she could try on some frames and order new glasses. Her eyesight was rapidly failing, and she loved to read and keep everyone up to date via text messages, or Facebook posts. Neither of which she could do anymore. So, I happily went up to fetch her.

We ended up taking her vehicle, because my air-conditioning wasn't working in mine, and it was a scorcher outside. She moved slow as if she was afraid of falling. Her balance had gotten worse, and I had to hold her as she walked. When we got there, I grabbed a cart in the parking lot to assist her in walking, and we slowly made our way inside. Trying on frames was fun and I could tell she was enjoying it. We even took pictures and sent them to her boys asking which one they liked the best on her.

When it came time to order the lenses, she was told that they wouldn't be ready for about two weeks. I think she thought she would get them in a couple days and told the woman that she might be having cataract surgery before they arrived. Well...she was advised not to order anything until after her surgery, because her vision could be extremely different. Which made perfect sense. I could see the excitement disappear from her eyes as she listened. She was realizing that she might not live long enough to wear the glasses she wanted. It was at that very moment I knew she wouldn't be with me much longer. My heart quietly cracked right down the middle watching her expression as the optical assistant explained.

We quietly drove back to her house without a word. To brighten her mood, I told her I could help her order some glasses online if she wanted and have them expedited. I did it all the time, and she would have them within the week. I gave her the website of the company I did business with, and she said she could have one of her kids help her. Now that I look back on it, she couldn't see, so how would she be able to choose anything online?

I began to leave her voice messages after that, because she could no longer read. She would send voice messages back and I'm so glad she did, because I can listen to them over and over just to hear her voice. Two weeks later, I got the call from her youngest son, to come visit because she was getting worse.

I still don't know how I braved sitting at her bedside that day. The last time I did this; I was eighteen as I watched my father wither away in a hospital room. But, deep in the back of my mind, I prepared myself just in case the day came, even though she would never admit that it could happen. I wondered how awake would she be? Would she be in a panic, scared or fearful? What will I say or do to console her? How will I act? Will I turn into a blubbering idiot and fall apart, causing her more stress? What if she is suffering and struggling for every breath? Could I witness such pain? These were legitimate questions you ask yourself to prepare for the worst day of your life. But when the dreaded time came, none of them mattered.

All that mattered, was I was there. Whether she knew it or not, I held her hand and stroked her hair. I kissed her forehead and whispered how beautiful she was in her ear. I thanked her for being the greatest friend I had ever known. I thanked her for her honesty and her shining example of humanity. She laid there motionless, but I knew she was listening.

The sound of reggae music softly pulsing it's beat mixing with sound of the oxygen concentrator, was almost like a quiet lullaby, emitting a calm vibe that I could have easily dozed off to myself. I noticed her mother passed out on one end of the couch, and I thought how ironic it was that her leaving this world was more than likely, more peaceful than her entrance. No chaos. No shouting. No crying. No panic or anxiety. Just calm and beautiful.

I would no longer see those beautiful brown eyes open. I studied her long delicate lashes and every freckle on her face as she lay there. The way her hair still shined with health, and how it fell perfectly on the pillow she was laying on. The small lines that were starting to form above her upper lip. I noticed every detail of her vibrant tattoos that she was so proud of, still as colorful as when she first got them. Her long, slender feminine fingers resting in the palm of my hand. There was nothing about her that looked sick. This was all so sudden, and I saw it as a gift from God. He spared her from severe weight loss, jaundice skin, and the use of an oxygen tank other than her last few days of life. She was gorgeous, even in death was my last memory of her.

I wasn't there when she took her last breath, but it happened only seven hours later. It was over. It was all a blur because it happened so fast, and now it was finished. All I could think of were her children. They adored her and were there for her every need in her last months. I never once heard them complain about any of it. What a wonderful mother she was. She did a great job raising those boys the way she did.

The planning of her celebration of life and her private service kept everyone busy during the month that followed. And when the day came, I sweated it out just like everyone else there. Only I had a revelation while sitting there. It was a moment that hit me like a ton of bricks. I decided that it wasn't over, and I wasn't going to let anyone forget her.

It has been five months since that day. Her birthday came and went. She would've been fifty-five. She would have partied like a rockstar. There would've been music and dancing. Her laughter would have been bouncing off the walls. The place would have been packed with friends she had made throughout her lifetime. People would have celebrated her and her existence. But they didn't.

I asked Alexa to play our favorite song, *Hips Don't Lie and* danced my heart out alone in my living room. With tears streaming down my face, I made the choice to celebrate her in silence. No one saw. No one noticed. I fought the urge to send her a funny meme via Facebook messenger. I wanted to fill up my newsfeed with pictures of her and go on and on about how I missed her. But I didn't.

I felt a wave of guilt. I felt as if I was cheating her out of the recognition that she deserved. I wanted the world to feel as empty as I did without her here with me. I wanted the whole of social media to feel the pain of losing her. The world deserved to be punished for forgetting her so soon.

Even as I write her story, I feel as though I'm not giving enough attention to detail. How do I paint a clear picture of what this woman was to me, without sounding like a lunatic? She wasn't God and no, I didn't worship her. I loved her. Not as a lover, but as I would a part of me. As I would a child. She was part of my life that I will never forget. She made it fun. She made it bearable. I know everyone says it, but my life will never be the same without hearing her voice or seeing her smile.

Her bravery and resilience in everything she experienced during her abbreviated life, is a testimony of how strong a woman becomes when you push her up against the wall. She pushed her way back away from it and just kept going. She had a vision on what she wanted in life, and she did it her way. The hard way. But she got there.

She died a successful businesswoman, mother, and mentor to many others that looked up to her. She died a friend to many. She showed the world that you didn't have to do things the conventional way. You had a choice. I wish she could've written her book about her wellness journey. I know it would've given hope to numerous people. And that's all she wanted to do. Spread love and hope to everyone around her.

She secretly planned parts of her private memorial service without anyone knowing. She picked the songs to be sung and the passages to be read. She always loved the huge sprawling catalpa tree we sat under that day and picked that spot to be the last time we all came together in her name.

Even though I questioned the audacity of some sitting there, I came to the realization that in some perverse way, she had a purpose in their life too. Even if I felt it was for all the wrong reasons.

People need people. Every life affects another life. For the good, and even the bad, people exist for one another. My purpose in life was to find her. Her purpose in life was to find me. Our names were written in the book of life without our knowledge, before we were even born. We were meant to be friends. Just as the people in your life were meant to find you.

Whether it is to teach you an important life-lesson, or to enrich your existence on this earth, your friendships matter. Tend to them and cherish them, for they will live on long after we are gone.

12

What We Remember

The holiday season has got to be the hardest time for many after the loss of a loved one. Things that we never bothered to pay attention to while they happened, come flooding back to us, as if they just happened yesterday, when they end. That is what makes a memory precious. They are once in a lifetime and will never ever happen again exactly the same way twice.

Most of our time that we spent together was at the bar that we both worked at. I pretty much worked every holiday, so she would go do her thing with her extended family at their house and end up downtown with me after her holiday obligations were fulfilled. I would always make some food for the locals that had no place to go, and she sometimes would bring her kids in for a bite to eat. Small towns are known for children in bars. That is where everyone gathers before, during, or after every major family event. No one ever looked down on it, because it was just a natural thing for us. It was the Midwest version of Norman Rockwell Holidays.

I don't remember her ever making a Thanksgiving dinner at home. I would usually have the holiday dinner at a later date, but she wasn't one to slave over a hot stove, so she always went to someone else's house for the holidays. I sometimes envied her for not making a fuss or stressing out over anything. While I was trying to be Martha Stewart, making sure everything was perfect, she just went with the flow.

I loved her for that. She taught me that you don't need to go all out. Just enjoy everything around you. It will still be a holiday whether or not you decorate a tree or prepare a family feast. Create some fun. Share some laughs. Her free-spirited demeanor, I'm positive, came from growing up the way she did. I can't imagine her mother planning a Christmas or Thanksgiving dinner. And her father...well, no. Not with her and her brother, anyway.

She used to tell me of some family gatherings with her aunts and grandparents on her father's side. They had a large family, so she said it was always a good time from what she could remember. I'm happy she had some childhood memories other than neglect and struggle. I can just imagine how precious she was when she was little. Those big brown eyes popping out of her head and her shiny chestnut hair falling around her little face. How could anyone cause such sadness to such an angel as her.

Her children were her life. And even though she went about things a little differently than I was raised with, they still had many happy memories with her. She saw to it. She surrounded them with only people she saw fit. People that laughed with her. People that loved her. She gifted them with sharing her friendships and they grew up seeing how loved she was by others. She shined like the star that she was when she was surrounded by people she felt at ease with.

She was my exact opposite. Nothing needed to be perfect. My "Type-A" fervor, blended with her bohemian nature and created an ideal personality. I don't remember ever feeling anxious or trying to prove myself around her. She omitted a vibe that filled the room when she entered.

I sit at the bar after my shift, and I make small talk to the people around me. But I can't feel the connection that I had with her. I know it sounds selfish and doesn't give credit to anyone else sitting with me, but it's true. I smile and laugh, trying to convince myself that I'm really having fun, but I'm not. I would rather sit home alone, than be there pretending that my life is just as normal as ever.

I see something funny on Insta, or FB, and fight the urge to share it to her messenger. I want to tell her the local gossip I heard while working, and realize I no longer can. I play a song that we used to shake our asses to and no longer see her dancing on her barstool from across the bar, telling the bartender "Turn it up!" I apologize to everyone sitting there at the time, having to listen to the same shit being repeatedly played on the jukebox every time we were out. I'm sure it was annoying.

I watch the same videos I have saved in my phone over and over, and recognize the hands, and the pack of smokes laying there, reminding me that she was always close. We were besties. We didn't want to miss a thing...together. We wanted to share the moment, in case Mr. Right walked in, or something funny was said. We wanted to experience it happening while together. She wanted to watch me fall in love with someone, just as I wanted for her. We never got to see each other walk down the aisle with the love of our life, but we got to experience more than one, "Mr. Right Now" moment together. I laugh my ass off just thinking about it. What were we thinking? We surely weren't in a healthy state of mind at the time. Hilarious!

Even though our life choices were more than likely, not the best, we still came out of them as survivors. We took a less than desirable situation and used it to our advantage. We learned from it and moved on. We never really dwelled on all our mistakes in life. We would laugh, shake our heads, and never mentioned it again. Unless we wanted another laugh. When we retold our version of what happened, it would get funnier and funnier every damn time. If walls could talk, our favorite spot would be the best storytellers this world could offer.

I could go on and on about all the things that she missed out on in life dying so young, but that would be weak. Sure, I would have loved to see her cry on her children's wedding days, and see her as a grandma one day, but I recall all the things that fierce woman accomplished in the short time she dwelled on this on earth. I know she left this earth a better place. I realize it has been said many times by many people, but when it comes to her and her amazing life, it holds true.

I am a better person. Her children are better people. Everyone she encountered is somehow better because she was in their life, even for a fleeting moment.

Life is cruel. She endured hardship from the day she took her first breath up until the day she took her last. But did she let it beat her down? Did she let the shitty things overshadow all the good things in life? No. No, she didn't. That wasn't her style. She fought with dignity and class until her very last breath. She even shared a laugh with me on her deathbed. I will always remember that moment.

I never met anyone that loved with all they had until I met you. You squeezed out every last drop that you had in you and poured it out on everyone within arm's reach. You were the definition of a good human. They are so few and far between, but I was blessed in knowing one in you.

I know you just went into the other room and still linger from time to time just to see what we are all up to. You haven't completely left us. I feel you near when I hear one of our songs.

I hear you laugh when I fuck up and think no one is watching. I see you still guiding your children through life. I see you in the snow that falls gently to the ground. You are the constant presence that reminds me I am not alone. I know I told you over and over how much I loved you, but just in case you didn't hear me...I love you.

Thank you for always having my back and seeing what I was capable of, before I even did. I will say your name every day. I will see to it that no one forgets you. You will always be the best time I ever lived, and my greatest story ever told.

Do Not Weep for Me (author unknown, re-written and edited by Tracy)

Do not weep for me, for I have loved and been loved by my family and by those who loved me. For I never knew a stranger, only friends.

Do not weep for me, for I have lived. I have joined my hand with my fellows' hands. To leave the planet better than I found it. *I have made a difference in this world.*

Do not weep for me, for I have not gone. I am the wind that shakes the mighty oak *and blows the weeping willow.*

I am the gentle rain that falls upon your face. I am the spring flower that pushes through the dark earth. I am the *beautiful, brilliant sunset that ends your day. I am the song that plays for you to remind you that I am near.*

Do not weep for me, for I have not gone. I am the memory that dwells in the heart of those who knew me. I am the shadow that dances on the edge of your vision. I am just around the corner.

Do not weep for me, for I have not gone. I will be there for your special days. I will be there for the births *and all the days after.*

I will be there when you reach out to touch another's heart. When you choose kindness. I will be there when you believe things are not going your way. *I will be there when you need strength and courage.*

Do not weep for me. I am not gone. But rejoice at the transformation of my being for I now have been reunited with those who have passed before me *and oh, how I have missed them.*

We will all be reunited again. Until then, live your lives to the fullest and hold your loved ones a little closer. I love you all. Thank you for walking me home.

About the Author

Paula Julson is a new self-published author, who while diving into her own healing journey, has collectively published four books in the last four years on relationships and life lessons. She uses real life accounts and situations with a *hold nothing back* attitude in trying to help you along your own healing transformation. Honesty and bitter truths are the only way to get there.